KEY

CONTENTS

TRAIL LOCATION MAP

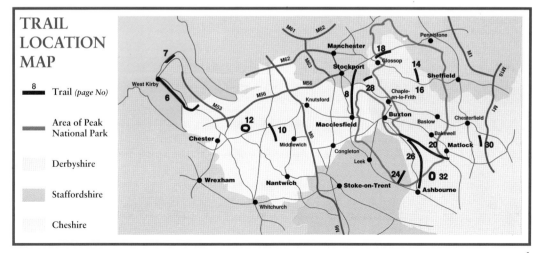

8 ▬ Trail *(page No)*

▬ Area of Peak National Park

Derbyshire

Staffordshire

Cheshire

ABOUT THE AUTHOR

Gillian Rowan-Wilde took up leisure cycling in the summer of 1993, her first trail being the Tarka Trail which she undertook during a holiday in Devon. Since then she has ridden most of the trails in the North West.

As well as cycling she is an accomplished fell and mountain walker and a member of the long Distance Walkers Association. Among her accomplishments as a walker, are the completion of one of the '100' mile walks, Mountain Marathons and numerous challenge walks over 30 miles.

She has completed courses at Glencoe in Scotland on rock and ice climbing also survival techniques whilst on the mountains with instructors from the Crowden Outdoor Pursuits Centre.

In this series of guides she hopes to bring to the leisure cyclist a catalogue of historical and interesting features on rides, together with some of the wildlife you may encounter.

MAPS BY

Andy Thelwell has grown up with Apple Macs and computer graphics. At present he is employed as a technical manager with a leading north west art studio

In his spare time he is either in the gym, or out off-road on his mountain bike.

ILLUSTRATION BY

Graham Nicholson studied illustration at Lincoln, since then he has been commissioned by many leading national, and international companies, supplying work for packaging, advertising campaigns and corporate brochures.

In his leisure time he is a keen walker, an interest he shares with his family.

INTRODUCTION

There is no better antidote to the noise and danger of riding on Britain's crowded roads than to cycle along the fabulous network of bridle ways, forest trails and linear parks that crisscross our countryside. Some are well known, some almost secret, but all have their own unique character to surprise and delight you - and in an environment well away from busy roads. Our series of guides is designed to show you how to make the best of these routes, the majority of which are off-road.

In this first guide we've chosen a selection of the very best almost traffic-free routes from the Peak District, Derbyshire and Cheshire. These are not 'mountain' rides, but enjoyable journeys for the whole family to take at whatever pace and time you wish. Each route has its own custom-drawn map showing everything you need to know, from distances and directions to parking, picnic and rest stops.

To guide you into the swing of things, we've also illustrated each route with some of the animals and plants you might spot along the wayside.

Thousands of people, young and old, are discovering the pleasures of off-road cycling, thanks to the comfort and reliability of the mountain bike. Not only is there the joy of seeing the countryside in close-up, it also offers a real boost to your health and well-being, even if you're the gentlest of cyclists.

If you haven't tried it yet, you don't even have to own a bike to start. We've included a listing of all the cycle hire centres on or near the routes, where you can try off-road cycling by the hour or the day. Be warned, though. Once you start, you'll be hooked for life...

Happy trails

Peter Gildersleve

WHAT TO WEAR - SUMMER OR WINTER

We all know just how unpredictable our weather can be, you may begin your day warm, and within hours be very cold. The best way to prepare for any eventuality is to layer your clothing so that as the day progresses you can maintain a balance between being either too hot or too cold.

Your first layer, should be made from a fabric that takes the moisture away from your body so that you don't get that cold clammy feeling, as you do when wearing a cotton t-shirt. The next layer must be a warm one preferably a fleece with a longer 'tail' to keep your back warm as you bend over the handlebars. Your trousers should not be too baggy otherwise the leg fabric could get caught up in your cycle chain. Padded cycling shorts and underwear are available, ideal for a day in the saddle.

A windproof jacket is essential as it keeps the wind chill away, since they are made of light weight fabric they can easily be tucked away in a pocket or small bag. Your waterproof layer should comprise of both jacket and trousers preferably made from a breathable fabric.

Mittens or gloves which have a padded palm help absorb the shocks of the bumps and of course a well fitting helmet is essential.

PACKING YOUR ESSENTIALS

There are various packs, bags and panniers available today in fact for some it can be difficult to know what to use and where to carry them.

Illustrated are a number of carrying positions for different capacities of bags. In addition to these there are a variety of touring front and rear panniers available. Coming from a walking background I prefer to use a small daysac in which I carry my food and waterproofs with a bar bag on the bike which usually has my tool kit, chocolate, maps and camera. Other people I know prefer to keep their body free and carry everything on their bikes - so you should do which ever feels comfortable.

Bar Bag • Bum Bag • Rucksack

Bar Bag • Rack Pack

Stem Bag • Wedge Bag • Seat Bag

WIRRAL WAY

The Wirral Way is situated in the Wirral Country Park, from West Kirby in the Wirral to Hooton Station in Cheshire. With the River Dee Estuary to the west of you and the A540 road to the east.

The Wirral Country Park was opened in 1973 as the first Country Park in Britain. The track of the Way follows the route of the old railway line which was completed in 1886. West Kirby to Parkgate the Way has a designated horse/cycle path and separate footpath. Parkgate to Hooton Station the route is on the Bridleway. *(The path can be very muddy and very hard going if it has rained)*

START:	East of the West Kirby Railway Station off the A540 **S**
FINISH:	Hooton Station on the B5133.
MAP:	O.S. Landranger Series No. 108, (Liverpool & Area), No. 117 (Chester Wrexham & Area)
LENGTH (approx):	19 ¼ km(12 m) West Kirby to Parkgate 13 km (8m) Parkgate to Hooton Station 6 ¼ km (4m)
SURFACE:	Hardcore, Grass
RIDE RATING :	Easy

NOTE If you are considering bird watching on the sands of the Estuary, do not forget to ask about the times of high tides.

KILOMETRES   1   2   3   4
STATUTE MILES   1   2   3

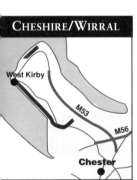

The first 8 miles of the route lie very near to the Dee Estuary with its scenery of sand, sea and marsh, looking westward over the water to North Wales and the Snowdonia National Park. The last 4 miles of the trail curves inland towards Hooton Station and the quieter sheltered woodland areas.

From West Kirby to Neston there are twelve bridges which, all bar one, have their names carved on a plaque under the arch. A deep cutting has been hewn out of the rock near Hadlow Station, so that the railway track could pass through with only a slight up-hill climb. When the railway was completed it was used to bring holiday makers to the coast. This continued until the Estuary began to silt up.

Up until 1926 Wirral Colliery was the main user of the line. After the colliery closed the RAF at West Kirby and the Ordnance Factory at Hooton continued to use the line until it eventually closed in 1962.

Several of the old platforms are still in existence, together with (A) Hadlow Station and signal box which were renovated to their 1950's condition, including a Waiting Room and a rack of old tickets and coinage, these include old pennies and threepenny pieces that can be seen through the Ticket Office window.

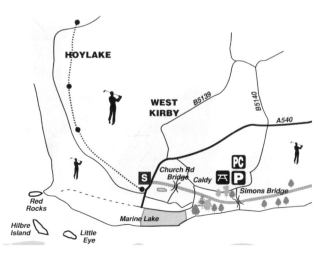

6

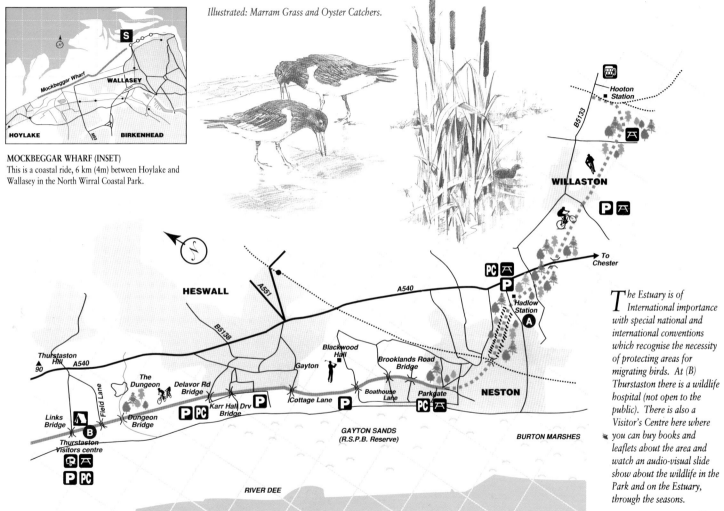

Illustrated: Marram Grass and Oyster Catchers.

MOCKBEGGAR WHARF (INSET)
This is a coastal ride, 6 km (4m) between Hoylake and
Wallasey in the North Wirral Coastal Park.

*T*he Estuary is of
International importance
with special national and
international conventions
which recognise the necessity
of protecting areas for
migrating birds. At (B)
Thurstaston there is a wildlife
hospital (not open to the
public). There is also a
Visitor's Centre here where
you can buy books and
leaflets about the area and
watch an audio-visual slide
show about the wildlife in the
Park and on the Estuary,
through the seasons.

7

MIDDLEWOOD WAY

THIS TRAIL IS LOCATED BETWEEN MACCLESFIELD IN NORTH EASTERN CHESHIRE AND
MARPLE IN GREATER MANCHESTER, FOLLOWING THE ROUTE OF THE OLD RAILWAY
LINKING MACCLESFIELD, BOLLINGTON AND MARPLE.

The Middlewood Way was opened in 1985 for walkers, cyclists and
horse-riders and follows the route of the old railway. The Railway line
opened in 1869 for carrying mainly coal, cotton and silk eventually closing in
1970. The Way is split for walkers and horses but, where the path is shared,
pedestrians have right of way.

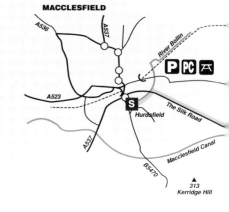

The trail has many contrasting views from the suburbs of the towns to the open countryside, from the canal as it winds its way beside the trail to the high ridges of (A) Kerridge Hill near Bollington and the flat wet-lands of the Cheshire plains.

Two of the old barge wharfs on the canal have been turned into marinas where, during the summer months, there are many brightly painted narrow boats passing through. The old working barges used to carry silk and cotton from Macclesfield, coal from the collieries at Poynton and stone for ornamental use from the quarries at Kerridge Hill outside Bollington.

The old station of Higher Poynton is an excellent place for a picnic before riding over the (B) Buxton to Manchester railway line and under the A6 to the site of the old High Lane Station. Nearing the end of the trail there is a sign showing the 'Rosehill-Middlewood-Macclesfield Linear Routeway' before reaching Marple and (C) Rosehill Railway Station.

START: Macclesfield **S**

NOTE:The beginning of the Trail is not easily defined, although it commences by the Bus and Coach Station in Macclesfield. Since there is a busy road to cross, it is easier to start your ride by turning off the dual carriageway ('The Silk Road') down beside the new Tesco's Supermarket, onto the towpath by the River Bollin.

FINISH: Marple

MAP: O.S. Landranger No. 118 (Stoke-on-Trent & Macclesfield) and O.S. Landranger No. 109 (Manchester)

LENGTH (approx): 17 km (11 miles) Linear

SURFACE: Cinders, Grass, Tarmac

RIDE RATING : Easy

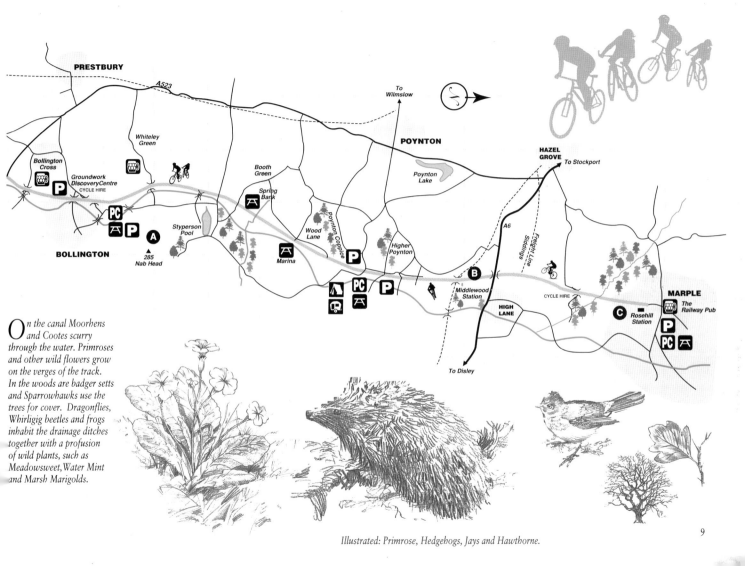

PRESTBURY

A523

To Wilmslow

POYNTON

Whiteley Green

HAZEL GROVE

To Stockport

Bollington Cross

Groundwork Discovery Centre
CYCLE HIRE

Booth Green

Spring Bank

Poynton Lake

PC

P

A

BOLLINGTON

Styperson Pool

285 Nab Head

Wood Lane

Poynton Coppice

Marina

Higher Poynton

A6

Freight Line Sidings

P

PC

P

B

Middlewood Station

HIGH LANE

CYCLE HIRE

MARPLE

The Railway Pub

C

Rosehill Station

P

PC

To Disley

On the canal Moorhens and Cootes scurry through the water. Primroses and other wild flowers grow on the verges of the track. In the woods are badger setts and Sparrowhawks use the trees for cover. Dragonflies, Whirligig beetles and frogs inhabit the drainage ditches together with a profusion of wild plants, such as Meadowsweet, Water Mint and Marsh Marigolds.

Illustrated: Primrose, Hedgehogs, Jays and Hawthorne.

9

WHITEGATE WAY

THE WHITEGATE WAY IS SITUATED SOUTH OF NORTHWICH AND TO THE EAST OF THE DELAMERE FOREST IN THE COUNTY OF CHESHIRE. THE TOWN OF WINSFORD TAKES ITS NAME FROM AN OLD FORD OVER THE WEAVER THAT SEPARATED THE HAMLETS OF OVER AND WHARTON, WHICH ARE NOW TOTALLY ABSORBED BY WINSFORD.

The Whitegate Way follows the route of the old branch railway line that carried salt from the mines north of Winsford to Cuddington Junction and then transferred onto the main Chester or Manchester railway link. Even in Roman times salt was an important commodity as it was essential for preserving food. The soldiers received half their pay in salt which they called 'salarium' from which we get our word 'salary'.

START:	(Sa) Winsford (to include the river section)	Sa
	(Sb) (An alternative start point missing the river section)	Sb
FINISH:	Ravensclough, nr. Cuddington
MAP:	O.S. Landranger Series No 117 (Chester and Wrexham) and No. 118 (Stoke-on-Trent and Macclesfield)
LENGTH (approx):	9 km (5 ½m)Linear
	(Sa) (3 ½ km from Winsford to the start of the Whitegate Way)
	(Sb) (5 ½ km from the Start of the Way to Ravensclough, Cuddington)
SURFACE:	Hardcore, Grass (Winsford to Whitegate Station)
RIDE RATING :	Easy
CLIMBS:	On the section from (Sa) to (C)

Our route commences north of (A) Winsford on the A5108. Turn left at the first roundabout down to the car park near the industrial area. Follow the path out of the parking area down the hill to the towpath beside the River Weaver. Turn right here passing the salt mine to your left on the far bank, going in the direction of (B) Vale Royal Cut. Once past the two ponds on your right, go through the gate where there is a picnic area on your right.

Over the bridge to Bradford Road, turn left up the hill, pass the main entrance to the salt mine on your left and a signpost on your right indicating the (C) Whitegate Way.

CHESHIRE

From Bradford Road to (D) Whitegate Station the path follows the high embankments of the old railway tracks giving magnificent views over meadows and moorlands of the Cheshire Plains. Whitegate Station is the only station preserved on this line with its platform still intact. The old sidings have been converted into a pleasant picnic area.

From Whitegate Station the track goes through wooded areas beside (E) ponds and water filled sand pits making ideal nature reserves for wild life.

The end of the route is at (F) Ravensclough beside the railway bridge, although you may continue down Waste Lane to the main road at (G) Cuddington

Although the trail is open to cyclists the path is split with a sign of a footprint for the walkers and a horseshoe showing the direction horses and cyclists must take. NB: (January '94 work still

KILOMETRES

STATUTE MILES

| 1 | 2 | 3 | 4 |
| 1 | 2 |

progressing on surface of 'Way' from Whitegate Station to Cuddington - this section can be muddy after heavy rain)

Illustrated: Fox, Cranberry and Birch trees.

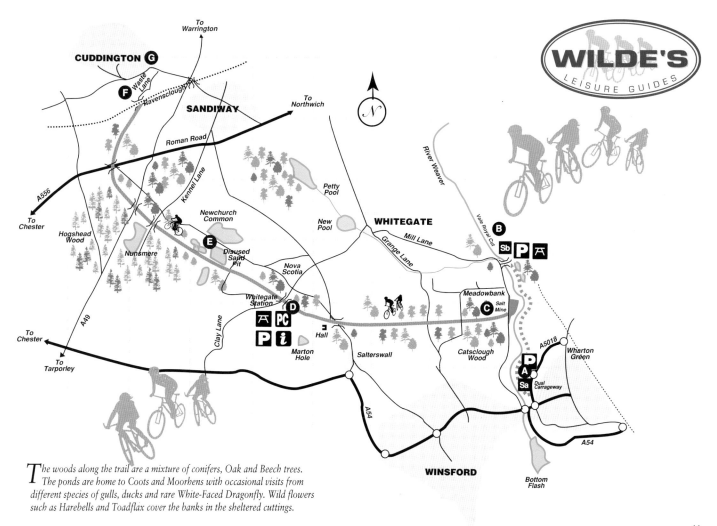

To Warrington

CUDDINGTON **G**

F

Waste Lane

Ravensclough

SANDIWAY

Roman Road

To Northwich

River Weaver

WILDE'S
LEISURE GUIDES

A556

To Chester

Hogshead Wood

Kennel Lane

Newchurch Common

E

Nunsmere

Disused Sand Pit

Petty Pool

New Pool

WHITEGATE

Mill Lane

Grange Lane

Vale Royal Cut

B

Sb **P** A

Nova Scotia

Meadowbank

C Salt Mine

A49

Clay Lane

Whitegate Station

A PC

D

P i

Hall

Marton Hole

Salterswall

Catsclough Wood

A5018

Wharton Green

P
A

Sa

Dual Carrageway

To Chester

To Tarporley

A54

WINSFORD

Bottom Flash

A54

N

*T*he woods along the trail are a mixture of conifers, Oak and Beech trees.
The ponds are home to Coots and Moorhens with occasional visits from
different species of gulls, ducks and rare White-Faced Dragonfly. Wild flowers
such as Harebells and Toadflax cover the banks in the sheltered cuttings.

DELAMERE FOREST PARK

THE DELAMERE FOREST IS IN CHESHIRE, SITUATED BETWEEN CHESTER AND NORTHWICH.
SOUTH OF THE M56 AND NORTH OF THE A54.

Delamere Forest is one of Cheshire's natural wildlife areas. The trails we have selected give you a choice of 3 circular routes along well made forest tracks of varying lengths.

START & FINISH:	Turn off the B5152 by the Delamere Railway **S** Station. Approx ½ mile to the Visitor's Centre
MAP:	O.S. Landranger Series No. 117 (Chester & Wrexham)
LENGTH (approx):	3 circular routes, averaging between 4 to 8 miles.
SURFACE:	Forest paths, gravel
RIDE RATING :	Easy/Adventurous
CLIMBS:	A variety of hills for the more adventurous

NOTE: For longer routes there are a great many tracks leading off the three that have been mentioned, but only ride on those paths that have been designated for cycling. Be cautious around the lakes as the peaty areas are very boggy and quite dangerous.

KILOMETRES

STATUTE MILES

The Forest acquired its French name from the Normans, meaning 'Forest of the Meres' and covers an area of 785 hectares. This is all that remains of the two great forests of Mara and Mondrum that once stretched from Nantwich to the Mersey.

CHESHIRE

M56

Chester · Middlewich

Nantwich

Birch woodland and shallow meres covered this area around 8,000 BC, along with Sessile Oak and Scots Pines.

Tools made from flint have been found in the forest thought to have been used by hunters as early as 3,500 BC. King Edward I appointed a Master Forester in 1237 and Delamere Forest became Crown land used mainly as hunting grounds by the monarchy.

The Forest has played a large part in history with the use of the timber for building, especially for Nantwich which was virtually rebuilt after their 'Great Fire' in 1583, by wood from the Forest given to the town by Elizabeth I.

The trees were also used for constructing ships and making weapons for the Napoleonic Wars. The forest was replanted with Oak seedlings in 1850 but the crop failed, and conifers were introduced to boost the growth of timber.

By 1869 the railway line was completed through the forest which by now covered only 2,500 acres. The Forestry Commission was formed in 1919 and began managing the forest in 1923.

Illustrated: Goldcrest, Bracken and Corsican Pine.

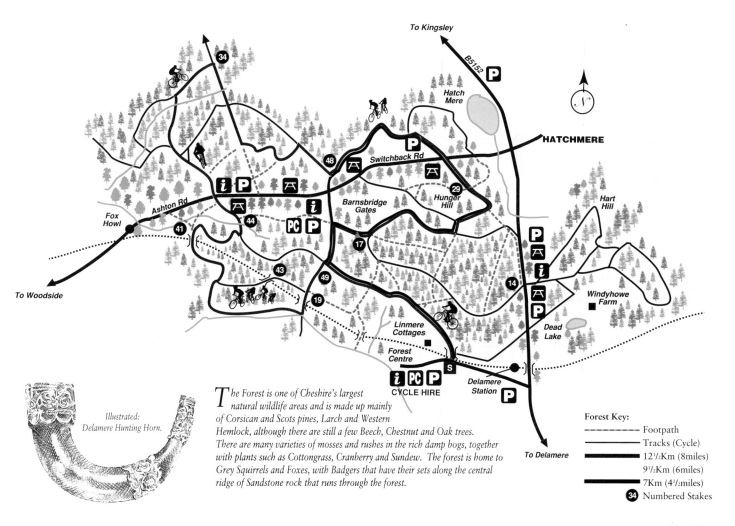

To Kingsley

B5152

Hatch Mere

HATCHMERE

34

48

Switchback Rd

29

Hunger Hill

Barnsbridge Gates

Hart Hill

Ashton Rd

44

PC

17

14

Windyhowe Farm

Fox Howl

41

43

49

19

Dead Lake

To Woodside

Linmere Cottages

Forest Centre

S

CYCLE HIRE

Delamere Station

To Delamere

Illustrated: Delamere Hunting Horn.

*T*he Forest is one of Cheshire's largest natural wildlife areas and is made up mainly of Corsican and Scots pines, Larch and Western Hemlock, although there are still a few Beech, Chestnut and Oak trees. There are many varieties of mosses and rushes in the rich damp bogs, together with plants such as Cottongrass, Cranberry and Sundew. The forest is home to Grey Squirrels and Foxes, with Badgers that have their sets along the central ridge of Sandstone rock that runs through the forest.

Forest Key:

- – – – – Footpath
- ———— Tracks (Cycle)
- ━━━━━━ 12½Km (8miles)
- ━━━━━━ 9½Km (6miles)
- ━━━━━━ 7Km (4½miles)
- 34 Numbered Stakes

13

HOWDEN AND DERWENT RESERVOIRS

The Howden and Derwent Reservoirs are situated in the North Eastern area of the Peak National Park in Derbyshire. Hope Forest lies to the west of the reservoirs and Howden and Derwent Moors to the east.

The trail takes you round the Derwent and Howden Reservoirs which were built between 1901 and 1916. These reservoirs help to supply the Derby, Nottingham, Leicester and Sheffield areas and between them they hold approximately 2000 million gallons of water.

START & FINISH: Fairholmes Car Park [S]

MAP: O.S. Outdoor Leisure No.1
                         The Peak District (Dark Peak)

LENGTH (approx):   18 km. (11 ½ miles) Circular Route

SURFACE: Tarmac, Woodland path

RIDE RATING :   Easy

KILOMETRES
STATUTE MILES

On leaving Fairholmes, cycle to the roundabout at the top of the steep slope out of the car park where the road goes to your right. This is a tarmac route that takes you through the forest. The road is closed to traffic at the weekend except for the minibus that goes along this side of the reservoir to (A) King's Tree. *Please remember to ride on the L.H. side as there will be other traffic using this route.*

At the north end of the Howden Reservoir there is a packhorse bridge at (B) 'Slippery Stones'. This bridge was originally in the (C) village of Derwent which is now covered by the Ladybower Reservoir.

Having forded the River Derwent at the most northerly point of the trail, the track back to Fairholmes goes mainly through conifer woods keeping close to the banks of the Howden and Derwent Reservoir. Eventually the road curves below the wall of the Derwent Dam and back to the starting point at Fairholmes.

N.B.:
Ride only on the designated cycle routes and not on the open moorland as there is no access on to the private land.

PEAK DISTRICT

Pennistone
Glossop
Sheffield
Chaple-en-le-Frith
Buxton
Baslow

To Glossop
A57

Bridge End Pasture

SITE OF DERWENT VILLAGE
C

Grindle Clough

LADYBOWER RESERVOIR

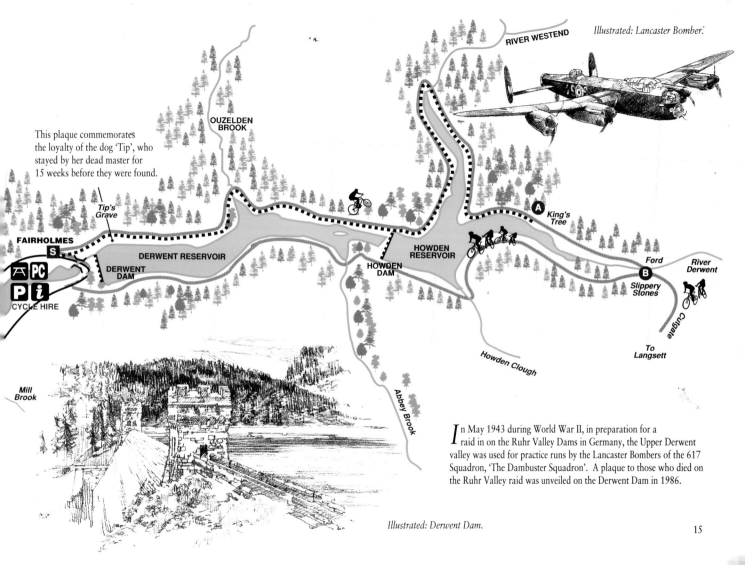

Illustrated: Lancaster Bomber.

RIVER WESTEND

OUZELDEN BROOK

This plaque commemorates the loyalty of the dog 'Tip', who stayed by her dead master for 15 weeks before they were found.

Tip's Grave

FAIRHOLMES
S

⛺ **PC**

P **𝒊**

CYCLE HIRE

DERWENT DAM

DERWENT RESERVOIR

A King's Tree

HOWDEN RESERVOIR

HOWDEN DAM

Ford

B

Slippery Stones

River Derwent

Cutgate

Howden Clough

To Langsett

Mill Brook

Abbey Brook

In May 1943 during World War II, in preparation for a raid in on the Ruhr Valley Dams in Germany, the Upper Derwent valley was used for practice runs by the Lancaster Bombers of the 617 Squadron, 'The Dambuster Squadron'. A plaque to those who died on the Ruhr Valley raid was unveiled on the Derwent Dam in 1986.

Illustrated: Derwent Dam.

15

LADYBOWER RESERVOIR
2 ROUTES (EAST & WEST)

THE LADYBOWER RESERVOIR LIES TO THE SOUTH OF THE HOWDEN & DERWENT RESERVOIRS, IN THE NORTH EASTERN AREA OF THE PEAK NATIONAL PARK IN DERBYSHIRE. THIS WAS THE THIRD RESERVOIR TO BE BUILT IN THIS VICINITY IN 1945, APPROX 30 YEARS AFTER THE OTHER TWO WERE COMPLETED.

It is adviseable to take the O.S. map for these trails as both these routes are more adventurous than the trail going around the Howden and Derwent Reservoirs. The climbs, although fairly steep to begin with, become fairly easy rides once you are on the moorland. It must be remembered that going over the moors can be very boggy, especially if it has rained recently. Spare food, a drink and waterproofs are essential in the interest of safety.

START AND FINISH	Fairholmes Car Park **S**
MAP:	O.S. Outdoor Leisure No.1 The Peak District(Dark Peak) O.S. Landranger Series No.110 Sheffield & Huddersfield Area
LENGTH approx:	12 km, (7 ½ miles) Both East and West routes are the same distance - Circular Routes
SURFACE:	Tarmac, Moorland
RIDE RATING :	Medium (adventurous)
CLIMBS:	Both these tracks have climbs.

KILOMETRES

STATUTE MILES

WESTERN ROUTE

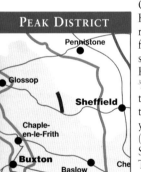

PEAK DISTRICT

Pennistone

Glossop

Sheffield

Chaple-en-le-Frith

Buxton

Baslow

Che

On leaving Fairholmes Car Park, ride along the traffic-free road on the west side of the Derwent Reservoir for about ³/₄ mile. As you begin to ride down the hill there is a signpost on your left for (1) 'Bridleway to Snake Road 2m'. Take this track up a steep ascent through a conifer forest. The climb does get easier as you traverse the hill. Keep a look out for black rabbits in this area. After (2) Lockerbrook Farm at the fork in the track keep to the left hand path and begin to descend keeping the woods to your left. On your left you will see a (3) sign for a track going down through the forest. This is a shorter way back to the road. The views are breathtaking up here, especially as you go down the steep hill to (4) Crookhill farm. Having gone through the farm, turn left and follow the road by the Ladybower Reservoir until you reach the turning down to your right which leads back to the Fairholmes Car Park.

Illustrated: European Larch, Foxgloves, Squirrel.

16

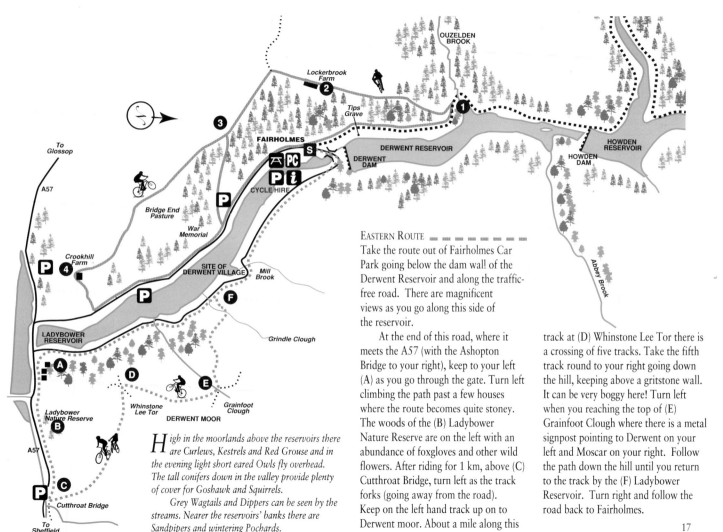

OUZELDEN BROOK

Lockerbrook Farm **2**

Tips Grave

3

FAIRHOLMES

S

DERWENT RESERVOIR

DERWENT DAM

HOWDEN RESERVOIR

HOWDEN DAM

To Glossop

A57

PC

i

P

CYCLE HIRE

Bridge End Pasture

War Memorial

Crookhill Farm **4**

P

P

SITE OF DERWENT VILLAGE

Mill Brook

P

F

Grindle Clough

Abbey Brook

LADYBOWER RESERVOIR

A

D

E

Whinstone Lee Tor

Grainfoot Clough

DERWENT MOOR

Ladybower Nature Reserve

B

A57

C

P

Cutthroat Bridge

To Sheffield

*H*igh in the moorlands above the reservoirs there are Curlews, Kestrels and Red Grouse and in the evening light short eared Owls fly overhead. The tall conifers down in the valley provide plenty of cover for Goshawk and Squirrels.

Grey Wagtails and Dippers can be seen by the streams. Nearer the reservoirs' banks there are Sandpipers and wintering Pochards.

EASTERN ROUTE
Take the route out of Fairholmes Car Park going below the dam wall of the Derwent Reservoir and along the traffic-free road. There are magnificent views as you go along this side of the reservoir.

At the end of this road, where it meets the A57 (with the Ashopton Bridge to your right), keep to your left (A) as you go through the gate. Turn left climbing the path past a few houses where the route becomes quite stoney. The woods of the (B) Ladybower Nature Reserve are on the left with an abundance of foxgloves and other wild flowers. After riding for 1 km, above (C) Cutthroat Bridge, turn left as the track forks (going away from the road). Keep on the left hand track up on to Derwent moor. About a mile along this track at (D) Whinstone Lee Tor there is a crossing of five tracks. Take the fifth track round to your right going down the hill, keeping above a gritstone wall. It can be very boggy here! Turn left when you reaching the top of (E) Grainfoot Clough where there is a metal signpost pointing to Derwent on your left and Moscar on your right. Follow the path down the hill until you return to the track by the (F) Ladybower Reservoir. Turn right and follow the road back to Fairholmes.

17

THE LONGDENDALE TRAIL

THE LONGDENDALE TRAIL IS SITUATED IN UPPER LONGDENDALE, THE NORTHERN PART OF THE PEAK NATIONAL PARK. (EVENTUALLY IT WILL BE PART OF THE TRANS PENNINE TRAIL WHICH WILL BE A ROUTE FROM LIVERPOOL TO HULL)

The Trail takes you along part of the route of the Great Central Manchester-Sheffield railway. It is a very picturesque valley, surrounded by high moorlands, which are often shrouded in mist. Whilst stretching out before you are the magnificent panoramic views of the Upper Longdendale Valley with the River Etherow and its five reservoirs.

START:	Hadfield Station, Platt Street, Hadfield,
FINISH:	Woodhead Tunnel
MAP:	O.S. Outdoor Leisure No.1 (Dark Peak)
LENGTH (approx):	10 Km, (6 ½ miles) Linear
SURFACE:	Hardcore, Grass
RIDE RATING :	Easy

Work on the railway began in 1839 and in 1845 the first passenger train went through using the newly opened (A) Woodhead Tunnel, which was 3 miles long and the third longest in the country. The line was eventually closed in 1981 ending 136 years of operating across the Southern Pennines. Whilst building these tunnels it gained dubious notoriety for the number of accidents and deaths that occurred. Many of those who died were buried in the nearby chapel of (B) St. James' in Woodhead just above the Woodhead Dam.

Along the trail, you pass a chain of five reservoirs that provide water, *nearly thirty million gallons a day* for the eastern side of Manchester. The reservoirs were completed in 1877 and were the largest artificial expanse of water in the world at that time.

There is a long history of processing cotton in various mills in the area. Most of the cotton mills in this valley were submerged with the construction of the reservoirs, although traces can be seen of the Crowden Bleach Works and the Paper Mill at (C) Fair Vage Clough on Torside Reservoir. Between Rhodeswood and Torside Reservoir, the (D) Pennine Way *(250 miles long)* passes on its way up to Scotland. You can also watch the sailing dinghies during the summer months, as they tack back 'n' forth on the reservoir.

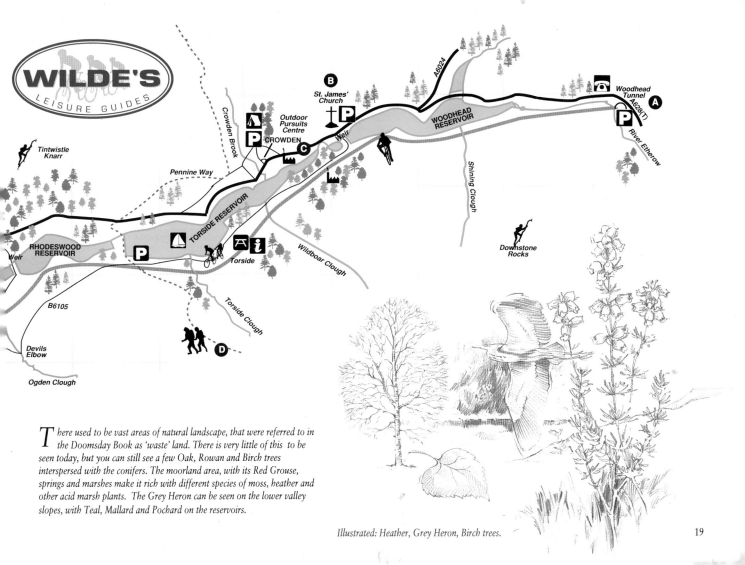

WILDE'S
LEISURE GUIDES

Tintwistle Knarr

RHODESWOOD RESERVOIR

Weir

B6105

Devils Elbow

Ogden Clough

Crowden Brook

Pennine Way

TORSIDE RESERVOIR

P

Torside

Torside Clough

D

Outdoor Pursuits Centre

P

CROWDEN

C

Weir

St. James' Church

P

B

WOODHEAD RESERVOIR

A6024

Shining Clough

Wildboar Clough

Downstone Rocks

Woodhead Tunnel
A628(T)

A

P

River Etherow

*T*here used to be vast areas of natural landscape, that were referred to in the Doomsday Book as 'waste' land. There is very little of this to be seen today, but you can still see a few Oak, Rowan and Birch trees interspersed with the conifers. The moorland area, with its Red Grouse, springs and marshes make it rich with different species of moss, heather and other acid marsh plants. The Grey Heron can be seen on the lower valley slopes, with Teal, Mallard and Pochard on the reservoirs.

Illustrated: Heather, Grey Heron, Birch trees.

19

HIGH PEAK TRAIL

THE HIGH PEAK TRAIL TRAVERSES THE SOUTHERN PART OF THE PEAK NATIONAL PARK FROM DOWLOW, SOUTH OF BUXTON TO HIGH PEAK JUNCTION NEAR MATLOCK IN DERBYSHIRE.

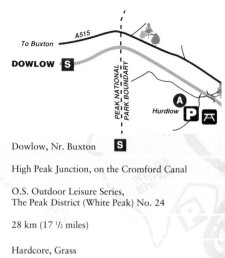

Josiah Jessop was appointed as the engineer to build a canal going north from the Cromford Canal to join the Peak Forest Canal at Whalley Bridge. However the porous nature of the limestone presented too many difficulties, and a tramway linking the two was thought more practical. The Trail follows part of the route of the old "Cromford and High Peak Railway" from Dowlow to High Peak Junction.

Work started on the railway in 1824, the first section from Cromford Wharf to Hurdlow was completed in 1830, and the second part to Whalley Bridge was completed a year later. It used to take two days for goods to travel the first section of the route which was approximately 32 miles (50 km) long and featured nine rope-worked inclines.

The waggons were pulled by horses on the level sections, and stationary steam engines using ropes pulled the waggons up the inclines. Steam locomotives replaced the horses in 1840. A passenger service was introduced in 1855 for the summer months only, but at the inclines passengers had to get out and walk. This service was discontinued in 1877, because of a fatal accident. The freight service was eventually abandoned in 1967 when the quarries ceased production. The trail opened to the public in 1972.

The trail starts at Dowlow, south of Buxton, on the boundary of the Peak National Park. There is no parking off the access road near Dowlow so use the car park at (A) Hurdlow and cycle up to Dowlow to start the ride.

Hurdlow car park is the sight of the old station which closed in 1949. It is approximately 4 km (2½ miles) down the trail to (B) Parsley Hay (your first picnic site). Where the views looking west towards the River Dove

START:	Dowlow, Nr. Buxton S
FINISH:	High Peak Junction, on the Cromford Canal
MAP:	O.S. Outdoor Leisure Series, The Peak District (White Peak) No. 24
LENGTH (approx):	28 km (17 ½ miles)
SURFACE:	Hardcore, Grass
RIDE RATING :	Easy, except for the three inclines which are fairly severe with gradients of 1 in 14, 1 in 9 and 1 in 8.
CLIMBS:	**Hopton Incline** - 457 yards long with a gradient of 1 in 14 **Middleton Incline** - 708 yards long and falls 253 ft with a gradient of 1 in 8 ½ **Sheep Pasture Incline** - 1,320 yards long varying between a gradient of 1 in 8 and 1 in 9. There were originally two inclines here, but they were joined together in 1857.

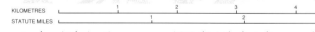

are spectacular. At the junction approximately ½ km past Parsley Hay, take the left hand fork *(the right hand track is the Tissington Trail, another day perhaps!)*. Shortly after this junction is the (C) Newhaven Tunnel which takes the trail underneath the

A515, this is the first of two tunnels you will be passing through.

(D) Friden Freight Yard was whe the goods waggons, having had a relatively straight run from Whalley Bridge, transferred to the smaller sho wheel based engines which

20

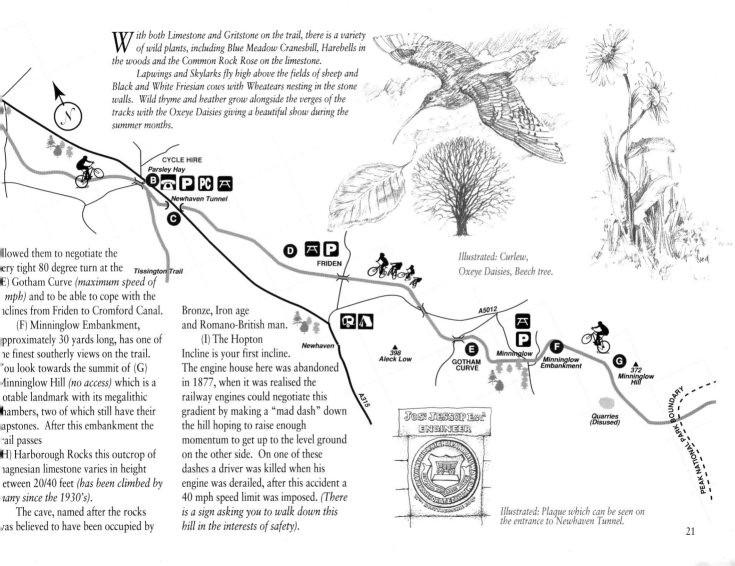

With both Limestone and Gritstone on the trail, there is a variety of wild plants, including Blue Meadow Cranesbill, Harebells in the woods and the Common Rock Rose on the limestone.

Lapwings and Skylarks fly high above the fields of sheep and Black and White Friesian cows with Wheatears nesting in the stone walls. Wild thyme and heather grow alongside the verges of the tracks with the Oxeye Daisies giving a beautiful show during the summer months.

Illustrated: Curlew, Oxeye Daisies, Beech tree.

CYCLE HIRE
Parsley Hay

Newhaven Tunnel

Tissington Trail

FRIDEN

Newhaven

...llowed them to negotiate the ...ery tight 80 degree turn at the ...E) Gotham Curve *(maximum speed of ... mph)* and to be able to cope with the ...nclines from Friden to Cromford Canal.

(F) Minninglow Embankment, ...pproximately 30 yards long, has one of ...he finest southerly views on the trail. ...ou look towards the summit of (G) ...Minninglow Hill *(no access)* which is a ...otable landmark with its megalithic ...hambers, two of which still have their ...apstones. After this embankment the ...ail passes

...H) Harborough Rocks this outcrop of ...agnesian limestone varies in height ...etween 20/40 feet *(has been climbed by ...any since the 1930's).*

The cave, named after the rocks ...as believed to have been occupied by

Bronze, Iron age and Romano-British man.

(I) The Hopton Incline is your first incline. The engine house here was abandoned in 1877, when it was realised the railway engines could negotiate this gradient by making a "mad dash" down the hill hoping to raise enough momentum to get up to the level ground on the other side. On one of these dashes a driver was killed when his engine was derailed, after this accident a 40 mph speed limit was imposed. *(There is a sign asking you to walk down this hill in the interests of safety).*

A5012

▲ 398
Aleck Low

E
GOTHAM
CURVE

Minninglow

F

Minninglow
Embankment

G

▲ 372
Minninglow
Hill

Quarries
(Disused)

PEAK NATIONAL PARK BOUNDARY

A515

Jos: Jessop Esq
ENGINEER

Illustrated: Plaque which can be seen on the entrance to Newhaven Tunnel.

21

HIGH PEAK TRAIL
(CONTINUED)

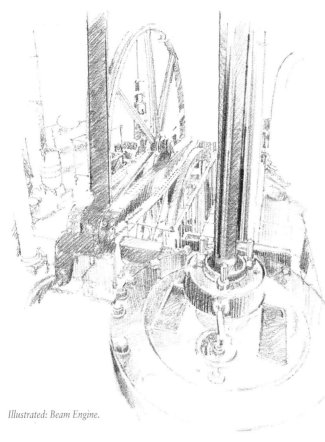

Illustrated: Beam Engine.

The area around the second tunnel at (J) Hopton, is a nature reserve, managed by the Derbyshire Wildlife Trust.

(K) Middleton Top Engine House, approximately 4 km (2½ miles) from the end of your trail, was where the waggons were transferred from locomotives to a pulley system in order to negotiate the steep (L) Middleton Incline. Inside the Engine House there is the last of eight condensing beam engines. Waggons were raised and lowered using two 14 foot fly wheels connected to a 1,670 yard length of wire, this ran on a pulley system down the centre of the track. As it was a double track the rotating wire would have the descending waggons heavier than the ascending ones, keeping them moving in a continuous circle. The waggons would be secured to this by using chains and leather thongs this method was used until 1963 when the engines were dispensed with.

On the Middleton Incline you will pass under an iron bridge built in 1825.

PEAK NATIONAL PARK BOUNDARY

Longcliffe

Brassington

(M) Black Rocks are a climbers paradise, with heights of up to 80 feet and overhanging buttresses of weathered gritstone. The views from the picnic site are quite magnificent looking across to Matlock and Riber Castle. Time to have a well deserved rest before you ride down to High Peak Junction and the Cromford Canal.

Sheep Pasture Engine House

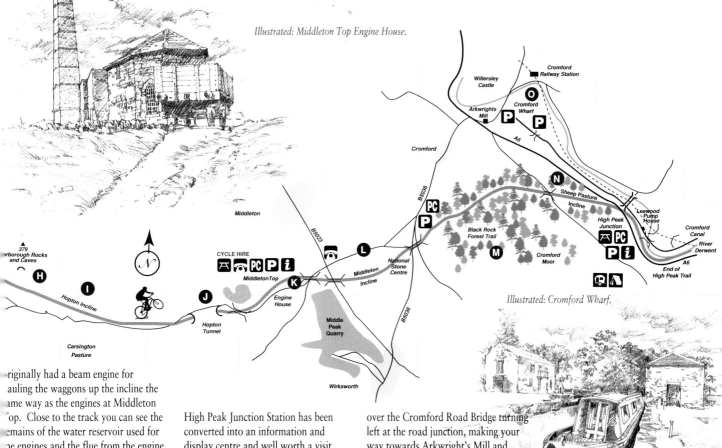

Illustrated: Middleton Top Engine House.

Illustrated: Cromford Wharf.

CYCLE HIRE

MiddletonTop

...riginally had a beam engine for ...auling the waggons up the incline the ...ame way as the engines at Middleton ...op. Close to the track you can see the ...emains of the water reservoir used for ...e engines and the flue from the engine ...ouse.

(N) Sheep Pasture Incline is a very ...eep gradient cutting through a forest ...f beech trees leading down to the end ...f the trail.

High Peak Junction Station has been converted into an information and display centre and well worth a visit. There are still pieces of the original pulley wire lying around beside the old waggons.

(O) Should you wish to finish your day at Cromford Wharf either cycle over the Cromford Road Bridge turning left at the road junction, making your way towards Arkwright's Mill and Cromford Wharf (approximately 1¹/₂ miles) or walk along the tow path to Cromford Wharf, ¹/₂ mile. *(Please note cycling is not permitted along the tow path to Cromford Wharf).*

23

THE MANIFOLD WAY

(meaning 'Many Folds' or 'Winding Valley')

THE MANIFOLD WAY IS SITUATED IN THE SOUTHERN PART OF
THE PEAK NATIONAL PARK, IN STAFFORDSHIRE.

The Manifold Way winds its way beside the Rivers Hamps and Manifold.
This track was once the route used by the Manifold Light Railway
(1904-1935) to carry goods between the villages in the valley. The valley has
great natural beauty. The limestone rock along the steep sides of the valley
contrasts with the softer sandstone rock and broader banks of the
River Manifold as it reaches Hulme End.

The River Hamps (meaning 'dry summer'). Often dry revealing boulders and the large leaved Butterbur plants.

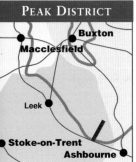

This occurs when the season has been particularly dry and the limestone rock in the River Hamps, near the village of (A) Waterfall, has allowed the water to seep down 'swallets' or 'shake holes' in the river bed disappearing into an underground stream running under Musden Low hill towards Ilam Hall. The River Manifold does the same disappearing trick by going underground just after (B) Wettonmill and reappearing in a 'Boil' Hole underneath Ilam Hall.

Where the River Hamps joins the River Manifold, there is a high limestone crag called (C) Beeston Tor. At its foot is St Bertrams' cave. Where Saxon coins were found in 1934. Following the trail beside the Manifold River going towards Wetton Hill there are, amongst many smaller caves, (D) 'Thor's Cave' with its spectacular 60ft wide entrance, where evidence has been found of prehistoric man.

START: Waterhouses on the A523 Leek/Ashbourne road. **S**

NOTE : *On leaving the Cycle Hire car park turn right on to the A523, taking extreme care on this busy trunk road. Cycle (or walk on the pavement) for approx ½ km. On the left there is a sign for the start of the Trail.*

FINISH: Hulme End on the B5054 Warslow/Hartington road.

MAP: O.S. Outdoor Leisure No.24 (White Peak, East and West)

LENGTH (approx): 13 km, (8 miles) Linear

SURFACE: Tarmac, grass

RIDE RATING : Easy

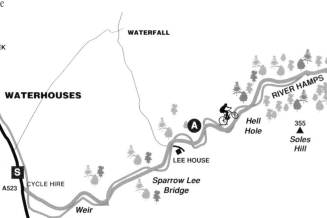

24

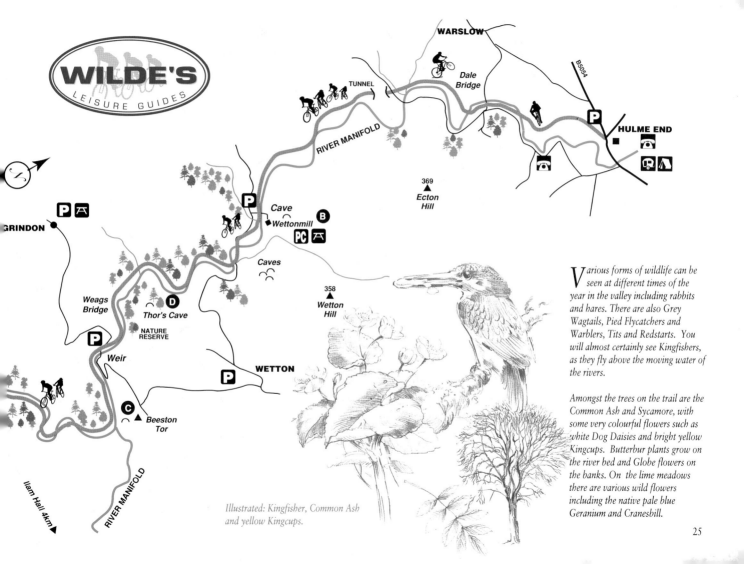

WILDE'S
LEISURE GUIDES

WARSLOW

B5054

TUNNEL

Dale
Bridge

RIVER MANIFOLD

HULME END

369
▲
Ecton
Hill

GRINDON

Cave

Wettonmill

B

PC

Caves

358
▲
Wetton
Hill

Weags
Bridge

D

Thor's Cave

NATURE
RESERVE

Weir

WETTON

C

Beeston
Tor

Ilam Hall 4km ▲

RIVER MANIFOLD

Various forms of wildlife can be seen at different times of the year in the valley including rabbits and hares. There are also Grey Wagtails, Pied Flycatchers and Warblers, Tits and Redstarts. You will almost certainly see Kingfishers, as they fly above the moving water of the rivers.

Amongst the trees on the trail are the Common Ash and Sycamore, with some very colourful flowers such as white Dog Daisies and bright yellow Kingcups. Butterbur plants grow on the river bed and Globe flowers on the banks. On the lime meadows there are various wild flowers including the native pale blue Geranium and Cranesbill.

Illustrated: Kingfisher, Common Ash and yellow Kingcups.

25

TISSINGTON TRAIL

THE TISSINGTON TRAIL STARTS FROM PARSLEY HAY ON THE HIGH PEAK TRAIL IN THE PEAK NATIONAL PARK TO ASHBOURNE IN DERBYSHIRE.

This route was the first railway track in the Peak District to be converted into a leisure trail (opened 1971). The trail is a very leisurely and comfortable ride with no hills to climb, except for a very slight downhill slope from Parsley Hay to Ashbourne.

START:	Parsley Hay - On the A515 from Buxton to Newhaven
FINISH:	Mappleton Lane, Ashbourne
MAP:	O.S. Outdoor Leisure Series No. 24 (White Peak District) and O.S. Landranger Series 119 (For the southern part of the trail)
LENGTH (approx):	21 km. (13 miles) Linear
SURFACE:	Hardcore, Grass
RIDE RATING :	Easy

The Tissington Trail follows the route of the Old London and North Western Railway from Buxton to Ashbourne, this was the last railway line to be built in the Peak District. It was opened to both passenger and freight services in August 1899. The freight service was mostly milk to London, and lime to Buxton, which eventually closed in 1965, although the passenger service had ceased during November 1954.

To the north of Alsop-en-le-dale, just below Johnson's Knoll there is the (A) Coldeaton Cutting, sixty feet deep and ¾ of a mile in length. (B) Tissington village is worth taking time to visit, as it is reported to be the prettiest village in Derbyshire.

Ashbourne has many beautiful old buildings built in the Midland red brick also the splendid Parish Church of St. Oswald who's spire is 212 ft high.

PEAK DISTRICT

Baslow
Chesterfield
Bakewell
Matlock
Ashbourne

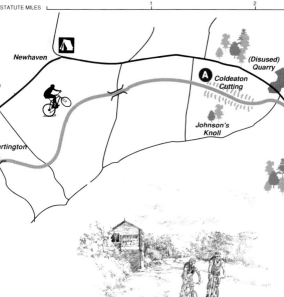

Illustrated: Hartington Signal Box.

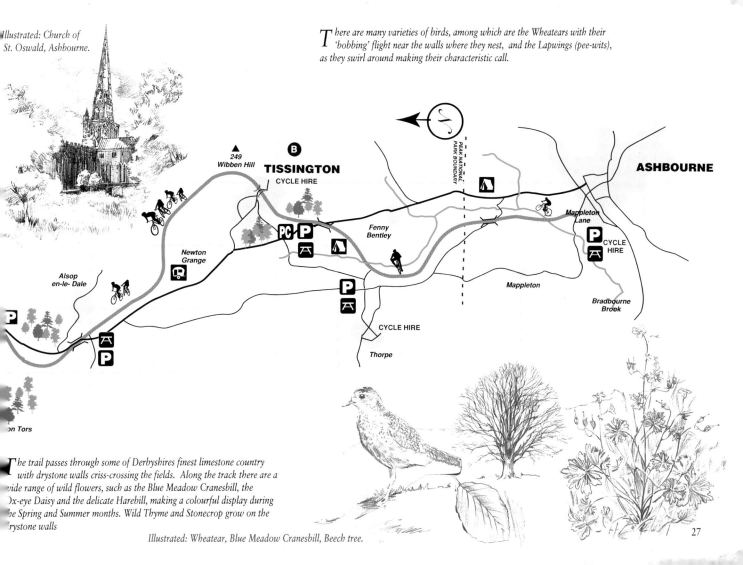

Illustrated: Church of St. Oswald, Ashbourne.

There are many varieties of birds, among which are the Wheatears with their 'bobbing' flight near the walls where they nest, and the Lapwings (pee-wits), as they swirl around making their characteristic call.

249
Wibben Hill

B
TISSINGTON
CYCLE HIRE

Fenny
Bentley

ASHBOURNE

PEAK NATIONAL PARK BOUNDARY

Mappleton
Lane

Newton
Grange

P CYCLE
HIRE

Alsop
en-le- Dale

Mappleton

Bradbourne
Brook

CYCLE HIRE

Thorpe

on Tors

The trail passes through some of Derbyshires finest limestone country with drystone walls criss-crossing the fields. Along the track there are a wide range of wild flowers, such as the Blue Meadow Cranesbill, the Ox-eye Daisy and the delicate Harebill, making a colourful display during the Spring and Summer months. Wild Thyme and Stonecrop grow on the drystone walls

Illustrated: Wheatear, Blue Meadow Cranesbill, Beech tree.

27

SETT VALLEY TRAIL

THE SETT VALLEY TRAIL IS DUE SOUTH OF GLOSSOP IN DERBYSHIRE AND WEST OF KINDER SCOUT. THE ROUTE FOLLOWS THE OLD RAILWAY LINE THAT WAS USED BY STEAM TRAINS FOR OVER 60 YEARS FROM HAYFIELD TO MANCHESTER.

The Sett Valley trail provides a traffic-free route along the former New Mills to Hayfield Railway, with its pastures and hedgerows providing food and shelter for an abundance of wildlife.

START:	Hayfield S
FINISH:	St. George's Street. New Mills
MAP:	O.S. Outdoor Leisure No.1 (Dark Peak) or Landranger Series No.110
LENGTH (approx):	5 km (3 miles) Linear
SURFACE:	Hardcore, Grass
RIDE RATING :	Easy

KILOMETRES

STATUTE MILES

The Hayfield Railway Line was built for the Midland and Great Central Joint Railway Co. and opened in 1868. The first locomotives to work on the Hayfield to Manchester line were the 0-6-0 Tank Engines. Class C13 & 14, the 4-4-2 Tank Engines, were commissioned in the 1900's. The line was closed in 1970 and was bought from British Rail by the Derbyshire C.C. in 1973. The old Station is now the Information centre and picnic area.

The freight that was carried by train was mainly coal and raw materials for the mills.

Around 1700 the increased demand for woven cloth led the people in the Sett Valley to start spinning and weaving at home to support their meagre agricultural income. The tall, three storey buildings can still be seen, with the weaving rooms on the top floors easily identified by their multi mullioned windows.

By 1800 the water of the rivers powered the spinning mills at Salem Mill and the (A) Garrison site at Thornsett. The dams that were built to help provide this power can still be seen. Due to these powered spinning mills the cottage industry with their hand looms declined very rapidly.

(B) Birch Vale Print Works prospered because of the clear swift running water of the River Sett and the introduction of water power for processing. Calico Printing was introduced in the 1750's but didn't really expand until the 19th century.

DERBYSHIRE

Manchester
Stockport
Glossop
Chaple-en-le-Frith
Buxton
Macclesfield

Illustrated: Bullfinches, Oak trees and Bluebells.

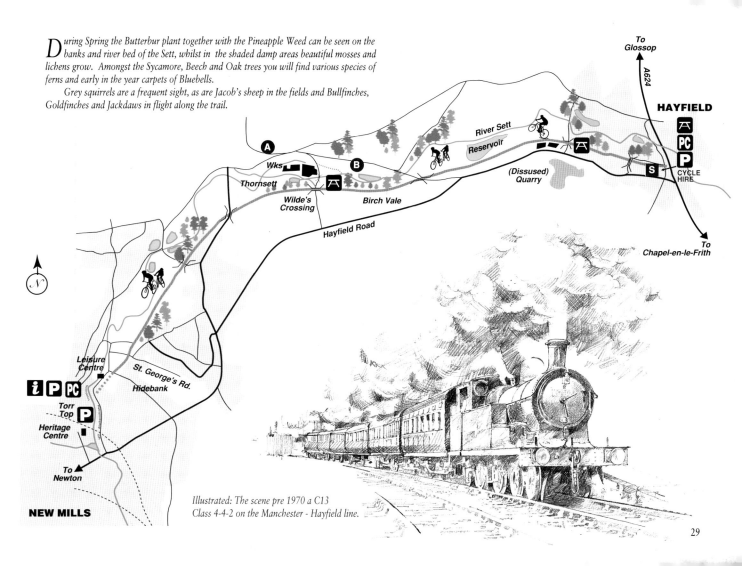

*D*uring Spring the Butterbur plant together with the Pineapple Weed can be seen on the banks and river bed of the Sett, whilst in the shaded damp areas beautiful mosses and lichens grow. Amongst the Sycamore, Beech and Oak trees you will find various species of ferns and early in the year carpets of Bluebells.

Grey squirrels are a frequent sight, as are Jacob's sheep in the fields and Bullfinches, Goldfinches and Jackdaws in flight along the trail.

To Glossop

A624

HAYFIELD

CYCLE HIRE

To Chapel-en-le-Frith

River Sett Reservoir

(Dissused) Quarry

A

Wks

Thornsett

B

Wilde's Crossing

Birch Vale

Hayfield Road

N

Leisure Centre

St. George's Rd.

Hidebank

Torr Top

Heritage Centre

To Newton

NEW MILLS

Illustrated: The scene pre 1970 a C13 Class 4-4-2 on the Manchester - Hayfield line.

29

FIVE PITS TRAIL

FIVE PITS TRAIL IS SITUATED SOUTH OF CHESTERFIELD AND NORTH OF ALFRETON IN DERBYSHIRE ON THE WEST SIDE OF THE M1 BETWEEN JUNCTIONS 28 AND 29.

The Five Pits Trail is a traffic-free route that follows the disused railway tracks and areas of re-claimed land. It takes in the old sites of the five main collieries in this part of Derbyshire. The route is undulating, giving splendid views from the top of the hills. Nature Reserves and lakes have been created out of the re-claimed spoil heaps, offering a haven for wildlife.

The Great Central Railway took over from the Midland Railway Company in 1892 to provide the five collieries with a means of transporting coal to London. By 1973 the railway became redundant as the coal seams worked-out. The land was re-claimed by the Derbyshire County Council.

The trail from Tibshelf commences on the site of the old (A) Tibshelf Colliery, where an excellent picnic area has been created. Once out of the car park and you have passed under the road in Tibshelf, the country side is open and hilly before arriving at the old site of (B) Pilsley Colliery. Cross over the road, along the track beside the woods at Waterloo and travel down the steep hill section through (C) Broomridding Woods. Follow the road round to your right, leaving the (D) Timber Lane car park on your left, proceed through the gate to a fork in the track. Keep to the left hand fork for the direct route to Grassmoor or to your right for a scenic circular route, going over Seanor Brook and past the site of the

old (E) colliery at Holmewood. Having cycled through the car park at Holmewood the trail takes you across the A6175, passing the (F) Holmwood Hotel and turning left before the bridge down to the road (keep the 'Bassetts' factory on your left), continuing on to the nature reserve and bird 'hide' which has been built on the site of the old (G) Williamthorpe Colliery. After (H) Woolfie pond you will meeting up with the track coming in on your left, keep right to Grassmoor Country Park which is on the site of the old (I) Grassmoor Colliery.

DERBYSHIRE

Sheffield
Baslow
Chesterfield
Bakewell
Matlock

START:	[S] Site of Tibshelf Colliery, East Lane Road, off Shetland Road. (Tibshelf to Newton road, turn left before going under the railway bridge)
FINISH:	Grassmoor Country Park

NOTE: *If there has been heavy rain the road is often flooded before you get to the Parking area on the Temple Normanton to Grassmoor road.*

MAP:	O.S. Landranger Series No. 120 (Mansfield, Worksop & Surrounding area)
LENGTH (approx):	12 km (7 ½m) Linear
SURFACE:	Hardcore
RIDE RATING :	Easy/Adventurous
CLIMBS:	The area is hilly between Tibshelf and Pilsley, around Holmewood and near Grassmoor.

KILOMETRES   1   2   3
STATUTE MILES   1   2

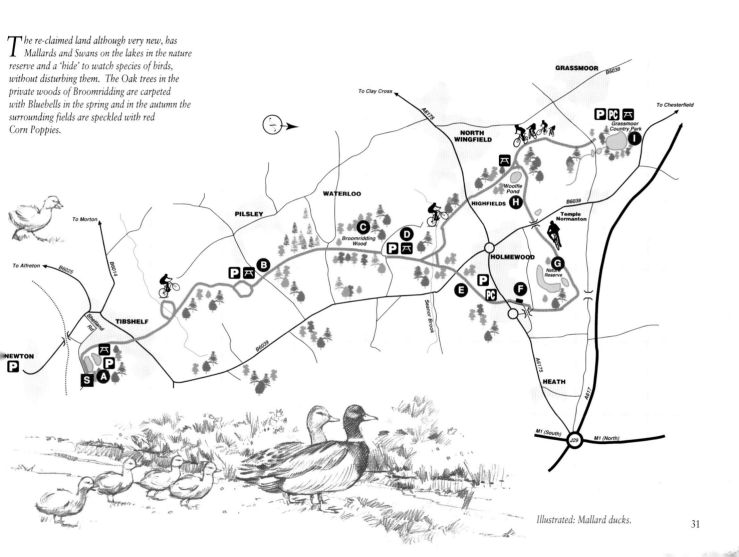

The re-claimed land although very new, has Mallards and Swans on the lakes in the nature reserve and a 'hide' to watch species of birds, without disturbing them. The Oak trees in the private woods of Broomridding are carpeted with Bluebells in the spring and in the autumn the surrounding fields are speckled with red Corn Poppies.

To Clay Cross

GRASSMOOR

B6038

To Chesterfield

Grassmoor Country Park

I

NORTH WINGFIELD

A6175

Woolfie Pond

HIGHFIELDS **H**

B6039

Temple Normanton

WATERLOO

PILSLEY

C

Broomridding Wood

D

B

HOLMEWOOD

G

Nature Reserve

To Morton

E

F

To Alfreton

B6025

B6014

Shetland Rd

TIBSHELF

Selmor Brook

B6039

HEATH

A6175

A6517

NEWTON **P**

S **A**

M1 (South)

J29

M1 (North)

Illustrated: Mallard ducks.

31

CARSINGTON WATER

THIS RESERVOIR IS SITUATED BETWEEN WIRKSWORTH AND ASHBOURNE OFF THE B5035 IN DERBYSHIRE. THIS LARGE EXPANSE OF WATER WAS ORIGINALLY THE HENMORE VALLEY WITH SCOW BROOK FLOWING THROUGH, BETWEEN THE VILLAGES OF HOPTON AT THE NORTH END AND HOGNASTON TO THE SOUTH.

Carsington Water was inaugurated by Her Majesty The Queen on 22nd May 1992. It is an area of 300 hectare, the third largest man made lake in the country. Planning for this project started in the Sixties with a view to supplying the East Midlands with the majority of their water.

START and FINISH:	The Visitor's Centre **S**
MAP:	O.S. Landranger Series No. 119 (Buxton, Matlock and Dove Dale area)
LENGTH (approx):	(Circular Route) 14 km (8 ¾m) - 6 ½km (4m) on Public Roads.
SURFACE:	Tarmac, Gravel, Grass
RIDE RATING :	Easy/Adventurous
CLIMBS :	Hilly in places on both Off-Road and Public Road Sections.

NOTE: The Reservoir is very deep, caution should be taken as the banks off the chosen paths are dangerous. Do not enter the water.

The Visitor's Centre is a building of immense presence constructed from local gritstone and limestone. A show piece has been built at the entrance to the Centre in the form of a spectacular system of troughs cascading water as though in a waterfall. The sporting and leisure activities around the reservoir are an asset to visitors.

One of the features that should not be missed is **(A)** Stones Island, near the Centre across the causeway. These Stones hewn from local gritstone and installed on the Island in April 1992 form a memorable landmark. The Stones can be climbed on and walked round, with the tallest pillar of stone standing 4 metres high. From the top of which you will be able to see various views of the lake.

On leaving the Visitor's Centre and going south you have a choice of routes, either over the hilly path by turning **(B)** right off the road before the dam or the path going along beside the dam. These paths meet before **(C)** Millfields picnic area.

The land around the reservoir is not particularly flat. There are hilly areas where you will be able to watch the different water sports while you contour the reservoir.

The roads from **(D)** Oldfield Lane are quite hilly as you ride towards the northern end of the Water, before crossing the **(E)** B5035 to the villages of Hopton and Carsington.

Once through these villages return **(F)** south to continue along the route back to the lake side and the Visitor's Centre.

DERBYSHIRE

Baslow · Chesterfield
Bakewell ·
Matlock
o
Ashbourne

KILOMETRES

STATUTE MILES

Illustrated: Flag Irises and Swans.

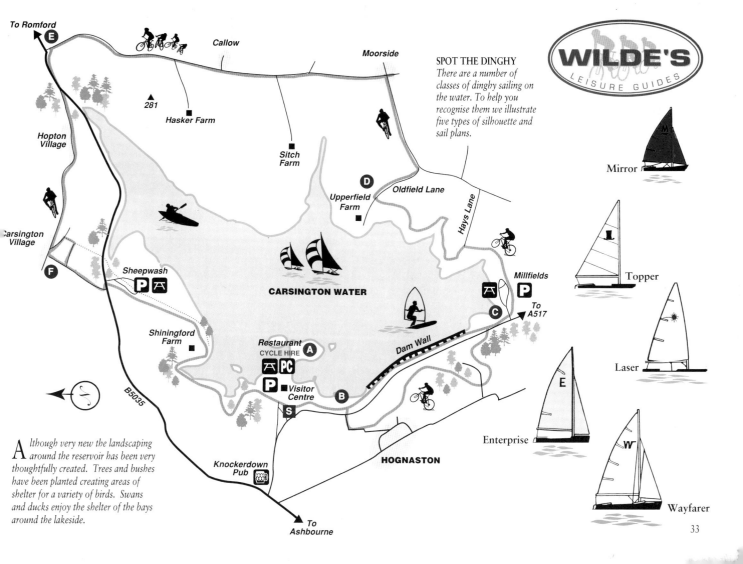

To Romford
E

Callow

Moorside

281

Hasker Farm

Hopton
Village

Sitch
Farm

D

Upperfield
Farm

Oldfield Lane

Hays Lane

Carsington
Village

F

Sheepwash
P

Millfields
P

To
A517

C

CARSINGTON WATER

Shiningford
Farm

Restaurant
CYCLE HIRE
A
PC
P
Visitor
Centre
S
B

Dam Wall

B5035

HOGNASTON

Knockerdown
Pub

To
Ashbourne

Although very new the landscaping
around the reservoir has been very
thoughtfully created. Trees and bushes
have been planted creating areas of
shelter for a variety of birds. Swans
and ducks enjoy the shelter of the bays
around the lakeside.

SPOT THE DINGHY
There are a number of
classes of dinghy sailing on
the water. To help you
recognise them we illustrate
five types of silhouette and
sail plans.

WILDE'S
LEISURE GUIDES

Mirror

Topper

Laser

E
Enterprise

W
Wayfarer

33

CYCLE HIRE CENTRES

The following is a list of cycle hire centres. Intending hirers should telephone for opening times and types of bikes available.

CHESHIRE CYCLE HIRE

David Bros. Cycles Ltd.
6 Cuppin Street
Chester
Tel: 0244 319204

Jack Gee Cycles
136-140 Witton Street
Northwich
Tel: 0606 43029

● **Macclesfield and Vale Royal
Groundwork Trust**
Discovery Centre
Linmere Delamere
Tel: 0606 40555

● **Macclesfield and Vale Royal
Groundwork Trust**
Grimshaw Lane
Bollington
Tel: 0625 72681

● **Oakfield Farm Cycle Hire**
Middlewood Way
Hazel Grove
Stockport
Tel: 061 449 0695

Pedlars Cycle Tours
PO Box 16 Winsford
Tel: 0606 592173

Sandbach Cycles
9 Bold Street Sandbach
Tel: 0270 764968

South Cheshire Cycle Hire
Meadow View
Crewe Lane South
Farndon, nr. Chester
Tel: 0829 271242

DERBYSHIRE CYCLE HIRE

PEAK DISTRICT CYCLE HIRE

**Alex and Luke Hatherall
Roughguide Mountain Bike Hire**
Wellcroft Filling Station
Peak Forest
Buxton
Tel: 0298 77059

**Alex Mackenzie
Mountain Bike Hire**
Staden Grange
Staden Lane
Staden
Buxton
Tel: 0298 24965

● **Ashbourne Cycle Hire**
Mappleton Lane
Ashbourne
Tel: 0335 43156

● **Brown End Farm Cycle Hire**
Waterhouses
Tel: 0538 308313

Buxton Bikes
Dale Road
Buxton
Tel: 0298 79880

● **Carsington Water Cycle Hire**
Carsington Water
Ashbourne
Derbyshire
Tel:0629 85478
or 0629 85648

● **Derwent Cycle Hire**
Fairholmes
Derwent
Tel: 0433 51261

● **Dovedale Cycle Hire**
The Old Orchard
Thorpe, nr. Ashbourne
Tel:033 529410

**Hartington Sheepskin and
Tweed Shop**
Market Place
Hartington
Tel: 0298 84459

● **Hayfield Station Picnic Site**
just off the A624 Chapel-en-le-Frith
Glossop Road

Inter Peak Cycling
Keith Hannah
Tel: 0332 76044

John Hart
Great Longstone
Tel: 0629 640507

● **Middleton Top Picnic Site
and Information Cenre**
Signposted off the B5036
Cromford to Wirksworth Road.
Tel: 0629 823204

Norton Barn Farm
C. Walker
Over Haddon
Tel: 0629 814195

● **Parsley Hay Cycle Hire**
Parsley Hay
Buxton
Tel: 0298 84493
(changing to 0298 484493)

Shipley Country Park
(signposted from Heanor and
off junction 26 on M1)
Tel: 0773 719961

Stan Fearn
Matlock
Tel: 0629 58289

Tideswell Cycle Hire
E.Jones
1 Market Square
Buxton
Tel: 0298 872118

● **Waterhouses Cycle Hire**
Earlsway
Waterhouses
Tel: 0538 308609

● **Tissington Cycle Hire**
School House
Tissington
Tel: 0335 25244

● **Cycle Hire Centre indicated on map.**

HOW TO ENTER FOR YOUR WILDE'S CERTIFICATE

As you complete each route fill in the form overleaf in the appropriate place. When it is completed send it together with a postal order for £1.50 made out to Gildersleve Publishing to:-

GILLIAN ROWAN-WILDE
Gildersleve Publishing Ltd
Capricorn House
Blackburn Road
Rising Bridge
Lancashire BB5 2AA

Name:...

Address:...

....

....

.... Age: ....

Signed: ....

Model of bike and date purchased:

....

THIS
CERTIFICATE
HAS BEEN PRESENTED TO

....

*For completing 17 off-road cycle routes.
The area cycled takes in parts of the
Peak National Park including areas in the
Dark and White Peak, Derbyshire and
part of the Cheshire Plain, also the
Dee Estuary on the Wirral peninsular. The total
distance being in excess of 160 miles.*

....

Signed

ROUTE	DATE RIDE COMPLETED	TIME TAKEN	COMMENTS ON THE ROUTE
1. Wirral Way			
2. Mockbeggar Wharf			
3. Middlewood Way			
4. Whitegate Way			
5. Delamere Forest Park			
6. Derwent & Howden Reservoirs			
7. Ladybower Reservoir Route A			
8. Ladybower Reservoir Route B			
9. Longdendale Trail	21.6.03	2hrs.	
10. High Peak Trail			
11. Manifold Way			
12. Tissington Trail			
13. Sett Valley Trail			
14. Five Pits Trail			
15. Carsington Water			

FAMILY ROUTE COMPETITION

You could win a Mongoose mountain bike worth £300. 2nd prize Fleece Jacket. 3rd prize a Giro Helmet

All you need to do is send us your own favourite off road route, together with this portion of this guide. Your route must be between 6 and 20 miles in length, be on bridleways or by-ways. If there is a road section it should be less than 20% of the total distance, and the ride needs to be easy to moderate. Please give brief details of your reasons for choosing this route.

The entry closes on 31st October 1994 and judging 1st week in December 1994.

The decision of the judging panel will be final and the results will be published in the mountain bike press.

Name:..

Address:..

....

....Tel:..

Please send to

The Competition, Gildersleve Publishing Ltd. Capricorn House, Blackburn Road, Rising Bridge, Lancashire BB5 2AA.

SEND FOR OUR NEXT GUIDE IN THE SERIES

Covering leisure routes in:

Lancashire
The Lake District
Cumbria

Due for publication at the end of July '94
(please complete overleaf)

Please send me the New Wilde's Guides covering mountain bike routes in Lancashire, the Lake District and Cumbria.

Please enclose a cheque or postal order (made out to Gildersleve Publishing Ltd.) for £6.85 which includes postage, and send it together with this portion of the guide to

Gildersleve Publishing Ltd.
Capricorn House
Blackburn Road
Rising Bridge
Lancashire
BB5 2AA

Name:..

Address:..

....

....Tel:...

38